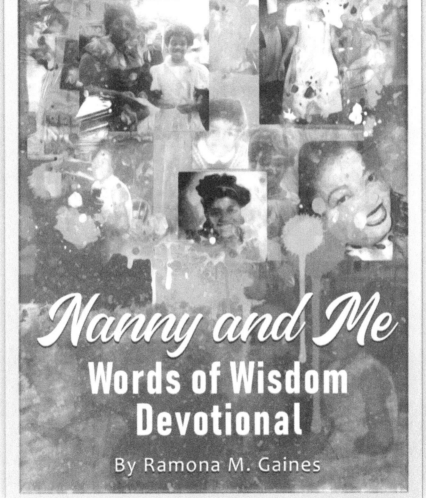

Nanny and Me Words of Wisdom Devotional

By Ramona M. Gaines

Published by Movement IS Medicine Publications a division of

MOVEMENT IS MEDICINE

ISBN: 9781097464968

Copyright © 2019

Printed in the United States: First Printing

This book or parts thereof may not be reproduced in any form, stored in a retrieval or transmitted in any form, stored in a retrieval system or transmitted in any form by any means-electronic, mechanical, photocopy, recording or otherwise-without prior written permission of the publisher, except as provided by United States of America copyright law

Dedication

Dear Nanny,

It's me your grandbaby Ramona. After all these years, I am still unpacking all that you instilled in me. It has been almost 24 years. I have done a lot of living, loving, and laughing and taken you with me in my heart everywhere that I went. Even Africa, the Motherland; I know, I know you said, "It was not your Mother's land. You always made me crack up when you would say that. Nevertheless, I made it there to a place I had dreamed of visiting and shared that dream with you on many occasions. We shared so much in a short period. Twenty-fours years never felt like enough time for us: I often felt cheated but then realized I could have never had you at all in my life so decided to give thanks for the gift you were and are for no matter how long I physically had you.

Once you transitioned, I was left with Jesus, my Word, and all of the sometime cryptic words of wisdom that you passed down to me. Something's I understood then and some I understood as I did what you said "Keep on living". Life has taught me a lot in the spirit of your "Keep on living" theory. Some lessons, I have embraced, some really challenged me, but they all made me into the woman, mother, daughter, sister, friend, and Woman of God that I have become. I pray you smile when you look down from Heaven and see your Grandbaby, "SweetPea". I desire to honor your memory and all that it encompasses the greatest being Jesus is the best thing that could have ever happened to my life. You lived, breathed, and walked this out before me in everything that you did. It comes out most of what I do and say to this very day. It is why I am writing even now.

Not long ago I was encouraged to write a book, called "Ella Mae Said". The reason was that I was always repeating something that you said. However hilarious it was it always had a ring of true and applied to the situation at hand. As I continued studying, my

Bible I even was able to connect it with the Word of God. So the earlier part of 2019 I did not think it strange when it was suggested that I write a Nanny and Me Words of Wisdom Devotional. For surely I had at least a month your sayings and Bible to be, a blessing to whomever would read them. It would be a labor of love and that is exactly what it has been.

So I continue to share what I selfishly tried to hold close so close I almost lost myself and bless the world with the prenominal you that you so freely poured into me. I understand it now; I was left to write the unwritten testimony of your life and share Jesus with future generations in a way that is palatable and easy to understand. To you Jesus was never deep or hard; He just was and still is that is it.

Until, I'll be loving you always,

Ella Mae Dunlap Gaines-Gibson
"Nanny"

Day 1

The Same Dog That Brings a Bone
Will Carry a Bone

Day 2

Nothing Beats a Failure But a Try

Day 3

Right Don't Wrong Nobody and
Wrong Don't Right Nobody

Day 4

Don't Tell Me What Nobody Else Did,
Tell Me What You Did

Day 5

If You Listen You Will Learn
Something

Day 6

Some People You Have to Treat with a Long Handled Spoon

Day 7

If They Talked About Jesus They Sho' Gonna Talk About You

Day 8

Corn Grows On Big Ears

Day 9

I Don't Have a Dog in This Fight

Day 10

Help Somebody

Day 11

It Cost You Nothing to Be Kind

Day 12

A Few Friends Is All You Need

Day 13

Love Will Heal What Ails You in Time

Day 14

Keep On Living

Day 15

It Must Be Jelly Cause Jam Don't Shake Like That

Day 16

The Day I Broke Her Heart

Day 17

No!

Day 18

After While It Will All Come Out in the Wash

Day 19

People In Hell Want Ice Water Too

Day 20

Either You are Going In or Out

Day 21

Prayer is Always in Order

Day 22

Don't Allow Anyone to Walk In and Out of Your Life

Day 23

You Don't Believe Fat Meat Is Greasy

Day 24

Put That in Your Pipe and Smoke It

Day 25

God Provides

Day 26

When You Mess Up Go to God and Him Alone

Day 27

Write Your Own Play

Day 28

I Want You to Be Like Her

Day 29

That Money Is Burning A Whole In Your Pocket

Day 30

Without God I Am Nothing

Day 1

The Same Dog That Brings a Bone Will Carry a Bone

Whenever I would come to Nanny with some information, that someone told me she would reply with this statement. My first though was what in the world does a dog have to do with this and second I was thinking what is the harm in having a little juice on somebody. Until one day, what I said to the person who gave me the information got back to me and I did not like it. I learned that day about gossip, and how harmful and hurtful it. I did not like being on the other side of that, coin and not that I have been perfect, but since then, I have been very mindful of bearers of any tales since then.

Scriptural Helps

Proverbs 17:9 ESV Whoever covers an offense seeks love, but he who repeats a matter separates close friends.

I Timothy 5:13 ESV Besides that, they learn to be idlers, going about from house to house, and idlers, but also gossips and busybodies, saying what they should not.

Day 2

Nothing Beats a Failure But a Try

Can't was a word that was not in Nanny's vocabulary. She would always shoot back at you and say, "How do you know you can't if you never tried"? Then she would reply with the above words, "Nothing beats a failure but a try. It is a quirky saying to say the least but full of encouragement to give the things in life that challenge you the old college try. That goes with anything you might be fearful about and not sure if you will succeed at it for example; auditioning for a school play, riding a bike, trying for a sports team, or interviewing for a job. You always should pray and put your best foot forward because it is true how would one ever know if they did not try.

Scriptural Helps

James 1:3 For the testing of your faith produces steadfastness

Day 3

Right Don't Wrong Nobody and Wrong Don't Right Nobody

Usually when I would try to justify a wrong action this would be Nanny's reply to me. Man would I get frustrated because she would always stand on the sides of truth and what was right. I intern wanted her to understand and to co-sign my actions whether right or wrong. Although Nanny loved me dearly, she never had a problem when it came to distinguishing right from wrong no matter how great her love. However as one grows and experience life you begin to learn that there is a right and a wrong way to handle things. Whether it be a disagreement or falling out; family misunderstandings and communication breakdowns there is always a right way for things to be handled. Even when one feels, they have been done unfairly or unjust. We should all work to be at peace with all men, whatever that looks like. God will deal with the rest not you.

Scriptural Help

Romans 12:18 If it is possible, as far as it depends on you, live at peace with everyone.

I Thessalonians 5:15 Make sure that nobody pays back wrong for wrong, but always strive to do what is good for each other and for everyone else.

Day 4

Don't Tell Me What Nobody Else Did, Tell Me What You Did

These were Nanny's famous words anytime I had become entangled in something. As children, you know we begin to ramble on and on when retelling a story. We start with what they did, then he said and then she said. Especially when we know that we are in the wrong, and we are trying to skirt around that part of the story for fear of getting in trouble. So Nanny would say to me, " Start from the beginning and tell me what you did not anybody else did". Man, you talk about feeling as if you were on the witness stand and being cross- examined by a fierce prosecuting attorney. However, you know what I eventually learned I'd rather endure being in here loving stern hands than a stranger on any day. Nanny's reasoning was if she didn't know the truth, she would not know how to help me. A lie would have here waste time and energy in an area that would not in the end benefit me at all. When in cover-up mode, we do not think that way but it is the truth. This lesson just did not help me when dealing with Nanny it translated over into my relationship with God. Just like his servant David when he said God, my sins are ever before me. Here is my stuff is what he was saying in essence. We can never get to our work if we are always dwelling on some else's is what this taught me.

Scriptural Help

Psalms 51:3-4 For I know my transgressions, and my sin is always before me. Against you, you only have I sinned and done what is evil in your sight; so you are right in your verdict and justified when you judge

Day 5

If You Listen You Will Learn Something

I struggled wit being quiet and listening when I was younger. I felt like I had a lot to prove and had to show off my intelligence. This was not good. One day while discussing something with Nanny she said to me, "be quiet and listen more". At first, I thought well if I were quiet, one would never know I know I know the answer. I eventually learned people don't always have to know what you know, and you learn about them if you are quiet. Sometimes people portray they are knowledgeable in a matter that they are not but are picking your brains. However, you do not learn these things if you are always running off at the mouth. These days I talk a lot less and listen a lot more.

Scriptural Help

I Thessalonians 4:11-12 and to make it your ambition to lead a quiet life: You should mind your own business and work with your hands, just as you were told so that your daily work may win the respect of outsiders and so that you will not be dependent on anybody.

Day 6

Some People You Have to Treat with a Long Handled Spoon

One day while speaking with my daughter I shared the saying, "Some people you have to treat with a long handled spoon". She asked what did I mean by that and I told her everyone does not deserved to be so close in proximity in your life. Does not make them bad but everyone should not be that close. That space is given to those who honor you are a person and are worthy of such a place. I shared with her as she grew, learned, and experienced life and people she would learn about such placement. Funny thing is one d ay she came back to me shared with me where she thought I needed to apply this saying in my own life. We went on a ministry trip with

Ms. V and it was very enlightening to say the least. Once we arrived back, home my daughter said to me, "Mom remember when you told me to treat certain people with a long handled spoon, and I said, "yes". She well you need to push that spoon a little further out when dealing with Ms. V." I was like whoa! I not only took her words under advisement, I acted on them immediately. They were spoken with too much authority and power for her young age. I knew if was the Lord speaking through her to give me a message that if I did not listen it would not be beneficial for me. I had given allowed her into a space that she did not need or earn access to in my life. We are never too old to listen.

Scriptural Helps

Proverbs 18:24 NIV A man of many companions may come to ruin, but there is a friend who sticks closer than a brother

Day 7

If They Talked About Jesus They Sho' Gonna Talk About You

Remember the first time you heard something that someone said about you that was not true? Remember how it made you feel? Angry, misunderstood, betrayed, hurt and wanting to retaliate to say the least. That is how I was feeling when I went to Nanny one day and told her that I had heard people were talking about me and that what they were saying was not true. Her response was, "If the talked about Jesus they sho' gon' talk about you". I was like but I am not Jesus. However, those words were preparation for life. She did not coddle me at all. They were words needed so that I could begin to grow thicker skin. Because the true of the matter is, people are going to talk about you. How you handle it is together a different matter.

Scriptural Helps

Psalms 101:5 NIV Whoever slanders their neighbor in secret, I will put to silence, whoever has haughty eyes and a proud heart, I will not tolerate

Day 8

Corn Grows On Big Ears

One day I walked in the house and began to have a conversation with Nanny and as the conversation began to progress, Nanny replied to me "Corn grows on big ears". In that, moment she might as well been saying to me, "Ancient Chinese Secret". That is what the translation of those words meant to me at that time. I stopped and stood there in the kitchen looking very puzzled. I did not know how to move forward or what to do so I continued to stare at Nanny and then she said it again slowly as if I would get it this time. Sadly, I did not but I did have enough wisdom to know to table to conversation and come back to it at another time. As I turned to walk, out the kitchen, I saw you younger sister in the adjacent dinning room looking wide-eyed and I said to myself, "Oooh". I then understood it was a conversation that she did not want her to over hear because she was not mature enough to handle it. It was of a sensitive nature and not age-appropriate. Just as Nanny knew what my sister could not handle so does God. He does not give us more than we are able to process and digest. He does not want us to choke like a baby that we are not ready to digest.

Scriptural Helps

I Corinthians 3:2-3 NIV I gave you milk, not solid food for you were not ready for it. Indeed, you are still not ready.

Day 10

I Don't Have A Dog in this Fight

Sometimes life places us in situations that do not directly affect us but pull on our heartstrings nonetheless. Many times, I saw Nanny take on causes that were not necessarily her's but she still felt passionately about them. She was often able to think what if I was in the other person's shoes. Although others often took the stance of the old saying, "I don't have a dog in this fight", Nanny still wanted to help those who were being treated unfairly or unjustly. I would that we would all think from that stand point, the world would be a much better place to live. Envision ourselves in the other person's shoes and see how we can advocate for them on their behalf.

Scriptural Help

Isaiah 1:17 NIV Learn to do right, seek justice, defend the oppressed. Take up the cause of the fatherless; plead the cause of the widow.

Day 10

Help Somebody

Nanny's house was often the hub of where things were dropped off in abundance and it was always more than we needed. It could be garden vegetables, bread; fish from my Grandfather's fishing expeditions, clothing, and the list goes on. Once we received it bags or whatever was needed to break it down and distribute the goods came out of nowhere and we began to break it down to share with those in our community. I became the foot soldier who was responsible most times for showing up at your door with this bag of blessings. Or if it was too late I had to get out the paper phone book and make calls for the neighbors to come and it pick it up. I laugh fondly as I remember walking down the street with a bag over my shoulder with one large blue fish that was almost the same size or larger than me. However, I was learning great lessons about helping others, that the world was so much better than I was. You see I never knew what the families were going through whose homes I showed up at with the bags of blessings but I was learning to help somebody; to be mindful of others and to share the blessings that God had so freely given to us. To some it may not be a big deal but to myself it is am important foundational piece that continues to play out in my own life today and I have passed down to my own daughter and she has began to practice as well.

Scriptural Helps

Matthew 25:34-45 **NIV**" Then the King will say to those on his right, 'Come, you who are blessed by my Father; take your inheritance, the kingdom prepared for you since the creation of the world. [35] For I was hungry and you gave me something to eat, I was thirsty and you gave me something to drink, I was a stranger and you invited me in, [36] I needed clothes and you clothed me, I was sick and you looked after me, I was in prison and you came to visit me.'

[37] "Then the righteous will answer him, 'Lord, when did we see you hungry and feed you, or thirsty and give you something to drink? [38] When did we see you a stranger and invite you in, or needing clothes and clothe you? [39] When did we see you sick or in prison and go to visit you?'

[40] "The King will reply, 'Truly I tell you, whatever you did for one of the least of these brothers and sisters of mine, you did for me.'

Day 11

It Cost You Nothing to Be Kind

It was raining and we were riding down the road. I was in and out of rem sleeps but I remember Nanny stopping the car and backing up. She offered someone that I was not familiar a ride to their destination. I was ready to go home and now wondered how much longer would this take since we had an additional passenger. The woman that Nanny picked up was so grateful and expressed this sentiment multiple times during our ride. I though wow this really meant a lot to her that someone though enough to see about her well-being and offer her a ride. Apparently, her car had broken down and she was in the process of walking home from work. When we arrived at her destination, she tried to give Nanny gas money and she refused to take it. They went back and forth for several minutes, the woman then insisted she use the money to purchase a gift for me. As I watched this from the back seat I got excited when I heard that last suggestions but Nanny refused that one as well. The woman eventually accepted that Nanny would not take her money and a thank you would suffice. That day I was proud to know Nanny and thought she was a really cool person.

Scriptural Help

Acts 28:2 NIV The islanders showed us unusual kindness. They built a fire and welcomed us all because it was raining and cold

Day 12

A Few Friends Is All You Need

Growing up I was an only child for eleven years. I have played enough board games against my own self to last a lifetime. Therefore, when I encountered others that were my same age or closer I welcomed them with open arms immediately. Some time too quickly. I spent so much time alone that for a while I always wanted to be surrounded by a crowd of people that I believed were all my friends. It made me feel important. One day a disagreement broke out amongst myself and my friends and people felt like they needed to pick sides. I who was once on the inside found myself on the outside looking in of the friendship crowd. Nanny came along and said a few words to me that I will never forget, "A few friends is all you need". I heard them but at that, time did not like them because I believed that I needed the crowd. Key word here is needed. As I grew and experienced life I began to embrace me and realized that Nanny's words were true. True in the sense of one you don't need anyone but God. In addition, that true friendships require work and maintenance. When one has so many friends, that task is an impossible one within itself. Besides in the grand scheme of this thing called life only a few will be there to endure the highs and lows, ebbs and flows of this thing called life with you. It is designed just that way. I no longer need the crowd and love dearly the few friends that I have and as Nanny said, "that is all I need".

Scriptural Helps

Proverbs 18:24 NIV A man of many companions may come to ruin, but there is a friend who sticks closer than a brother.

John 15:13 NIV Greater love has no one than this that he lay down his life for his friends.

Day 13

Love Will Heal What Ails You in Time

In this life, we all get wounded. There is no getting around it. It is sort of of a sickness of the soul thing that happens to everyone in their lifetime but many may or may not share or expose with others even those closest to you. You just go through life silently praying for God make the pain of the ache hurt a little less each day. As you move about through your everyday life and healthy love comes into your life, it does begin to cure what ails you in time. It does not happen over night but you can heal and recover. Nanny's love and prayers helped me to begin my healing process. It was the blood of Christ that wiped it away as I continued to surrender it all to Him.

Scriptural Helps

Psalm 147:3 NIV He heals the brokenhearted and binds up their wounds.

Jeremiah 33:6 NIV Nevertheless, I will bring health and healing to it; I will heal my people and will let them enjoy abundant peace and security.

Day 14

Keep on Living

I remember the day so clearly that I said this to Nanny as I was sharing a story about something with her. To me I made absolutely no sense and I was not able to wrap my head around something that someone had done. When I was finishing up my part of the story, I said to Nanny, "Well I never", and her reply was, "keep on living". I looked at her in shock as if to say there can't be more bizarre things like this to come in life. Surely, people are not this impetuous and silly. Guess what they are and it does and can get worse. Even in my own life I have had my own thoughts are feelings that fell into the "well I never" category as well, yes even me. We have moments and go through different experiences. They are the things that grow and mature us into who we are. Life is a great teacher so keep on living and learning the lessons that come along with it.

Scriptural Helps

Ephesians 5:15-16 NIV Be very careful, then, how you live-not as unwise but as wise, making the most of every opportunity, because the days are evil.

Proverbs 10:17 NIV Whoever heeds discipline shows the way to life, but whoever ignores correction leads others astray

Day 15

It Must Be Jelly Cause Jam Don't Shake Like That

When I left home, went away to college, and came back I had gained some weight. When I left for school, I was a cool 126 and had maintained that for sometime. However, there are disciplines at home that you don't necessarily adhere to once you leave the nest. College is that place where you experiment with what you know versus what you learn once you get there and see what works for you. In more ways than one to say the least but I digress. On one of my visits, home I accompanied Nanny to her place of work and I met her co-workers and I remember her looking at me and saying, "It must be jelly cause jam don't shake like that". I was like what in the world is she talking about? Then one of her co-workers said to her to leave me alone the weight looked fine on me. We never discussed my weight before and I don't even think until that day I paid attention to it myself. Nanny then said to me, " You better slow down with the food it will catch up with you in no time". I am not sure if all of what happened in this exchange registered at that time but eventually I began to try to make better decisions with my eating habits because of what Nanny said because as usual she was right. It did catch up to me in no time especially when you start to have children. However, as with everything, it is not the end of the world and we are a work in progress so never stop working on you. Jelly, jam, rolls and all....

Scriptural Helps

3 John 2 NIV Dear friend, I pray that you may enjoy good health and that all may go well with you, even as your soul is getting along well.

I Corinthians 6:19-20 NIV Do you not know that your bodies are temples of the Holy Spirit, who is in you, whom you have received from God? You are not your own, you are bough at a price. Therefore, honor God with your bodies.

Day 16

The Day I Broke Her Heart

I saw the tears, fear, and disappointment in her eyes. She did not hide and it from me. In that moment, I wanted to hide from me because I was already disappointed in myself that I had gotten in to this debacle. While away in college I was caught up into something that was very different from my character and who I was raised to be. Nanny had instructed me on how to handle it but it was going to cost her money so I thought I would save her money and do it another way. Me not knowing I had not lived long enough to know what the outcome could be. However, she did and that is why there was fear, hopelessness, and helplessness in her eyes. I knew for sure this was the day I broke Nanny's heart. Somehow, little by little we were able to recover from this moment. Her love remained constant and she made sure I was aware of it. It didn't break our bond if anything it made it stronger because it reinforced that I could trust her with anything and that her support in my life was truly unwavering as she always said it would be.

Scriptural Helps

Job 14 NIV 1 Mortals, born of a woman are of few days and full of trouble

Proverbs 29:15 NIV A rod and reprimand impart wisdom, but a child left undisciplined disgraces its mother.

Proverbs 13:1 NIV A wise son heeds his father's instruction, but a mocker does not respond to rebukes.

99

Day 17

No!

As children when we want something, we do not want to hear or expect to hear the words "No" from our parents or caregivers. Especially if you believe it is not a hardship. So I remember going to Nanny one day and asking for something and her answer was, "No". I was in shock. I don't remember ever asking for much so I could not believe that, "No" would be her answer to me. Not her precious Ramona, I thought. However, she said it and she meant it and did not blink. As time went on she said, "NO" some more and eventually I stopped going into shock and realized she had a right to decide what she would, could, or would not do for me. When I became and adult I understood she was teaching me a lesson. A lesson I would use with my own daughter as I raised her. Just because I can say yes does not mean I should. If I gave her everything, how would I teach her how to earn anything? It would also give her an unrealistic outlook on life. Nanny saying, "NO" taught me about perspective and discipline. It also prepared me to be a parent and to teach some invaluable lessons.

Scriptural Helps

Hebrews 12:11 NIV No discipline seems pleasant at the time, but painful. Later on, however, it produces a harvest of righteousness and peace for those who have been trained by it.

Proverbs 19:18 NIV Discipline your children, for in that there is hope; do not be a willing party to their death.

Day 18

After While It Will All Come Out in the Wash

As I am sure you can tell, Nanny and I had many conversations about life, people, places, and things. A whole lot of them. Talking to her was like being on a crash course of Life Lessons 101, 102, and 103. Always an adventure to say the least.

One day we were talking about a certain issue and we were both stating our viewpoints on whether it was true or not true. Her response this day was, "It will all come out in the wash". I was thinking to myself what does the laundry have to do with this matter. However, as I sat back and though out the laundry one day it began to make sense. Everything that you ever put in the wash does come back out, even the sock mates that we claim disappear magically. I soon understood it was not about laundry but really truth and how it inevitably does come out. No matter how long we may think it takes, it will. Something's we just have to be patient with and the process.

Scriptural Helps

Proverbs 12:19 NIV Truthful lips endure forever, but a lying tongue lasts only a moment.

Proverbs 14:25 NIV A truthful witness saves lives, but a false witness is deceitful

Day 19

People In Hell Want Ice Water Too

Every child goes through that infamous I want stage. So much so that you get the speech before you go into the store; you know the don't look at anything; do not ask for anything and please God do not touch anything. If you break anything, I am going to break you, so on, and so forth. All we know as children is that we want and that is all that matters. So one day I started my, "I want" appeal in the store with Nanny when we were out shopping. It was for a toy that I saw at Kmart. I think I thought I could eventually wear her down. Her next words threw me for a loop. And they were, "People in hell want ice water". I gasped because you could not tell me that hell was not a cuss word and that Nanny did not just cuss at me. I did not ask for the toy any more. I was too scared and did not want to make Nanny, "cuss" anymore.

Scriptural Helps

Ephesians 6:1 NIV Children, obey your parents in the Lord, for this is right

Day 20

Either You are Going to In or Out

On summer days these were every household's favorite words, "Either you are going in or out. Why because they were tired of us letting the door slam, letting flies in and if you had an air conditioner letting the air out. Those words are similar to our relationship with God, either we are going to be in or out, hot or cold. He never asked us to be perfect and that was one of the things Nanny always stressed to me. Your relationship with God is between you and Him. Don't invite anybody else in to that sacred space that that you and He have created and be in either in or out.

Scriptural Helps

Revelation 3:15 NIV I know your deeds, that you are neither cold nor hot I wish you were either one or the other!

Day 21

Prayer is Always in Order

The day before Nanny passed away her room at the hospital was full of visitors. I don't think at that point I had ever had so much prayer in a 24-hour period in my life. Everyone that came wanted to have prayer with us. I remember running out of the room after realizing that she had signed a DNR order, "Do Not Resuscitate". My grandfather had to ok it. I was not ok but tried to make myself ok. Nanny even prayed with me and kept praying for her soul. Her prayer was short and simple, "Lord have mercy", that's all nothing fancy. Nanny never did go to God fancy she went just as she was and that is what she always taught me; so even in her last moments here on earth she remained consistent in her prayer posture. The lesson remained the same as well; prayer is always in order in life and in death as well.

Scriptural Helps

James 5:16 NIV Therefore confess your sins to each other and pray for each other so that you may be healed. The prayer of a righteous person is powerful and effective.

Ephesians 6:18 NIV And pray in the spirit on all occasions with all kinds of prayers and requests. With this in mind, be alert and always keep on praying for all the Lord's people.

Day 22

Don't Allow Anyone to Walk In and Out of Your Life

When I was 20 years old I was in love and eventually got engaged to be married. I thought that he was the "One". However, we were both immature in many ways and allowed ourselves and others to get in the way of our relationship. We were on and off many times during this whole rollercoaster of love thing. One day I was visiting Nanny in the hospital during one of her many stays after she was diagnosed with cancer. She asked me about "William". I was like how did she know to ask about him. He was actually in the car in the hospital parking lot. She knew everything without me saying a word!!!! I lied and said I didn't know. She looked at me and said, "Don't allow anyone to keep walking in and out of your life". I said ok and awkwardly stood there in the truth of that moment. It felt like forever although it was probably only a minute. She was right but I had to come to things on my own terms and she as always respected that once she spoke her peace. This was not just about my relationship with "William" but in every other relationship that I would have in my adult life. I learned from those words that people don't just leave physically, but emotionally and mentally as well and I have a right to expect them to be present and if not to move on. It is not something I have to accept so I wont be alone. Friends stay when things are good and when they are bad. They don't pick or choose what they stay for they just do.

Scriptural Helps

Proverbs 17:17 NIV A friend loves at all times, and a brother is born for a time of adversity

Ephesians 4:16 NIV From him the whole body, joined and held together by every supporting ligament, grows and builds itself up in love, as each part does its work.

Day 23

You Don't Believe Fat Meat Is Greasy

We all have those times when we hear what the adults in our lives are saying but believe we still no better than they do although they have been here much longer. They have the benefit of experience wisdom of others to draw from and are trying to keep us from hitting the same brick walls that they hit or saw others hit. I remember the day I attempted to talk Nanny out of what she really knew and convince her that I knew so much better. As usual, it was about a guy, and as usual she was right but I wanted her to be wrong. Her famous last words, "Were go ahead and do what you want to do because you don't believe fat meat is greasy". Fat and meat and grease, really Nanny were my thoughts but I was not crazy enough to say it aloud. I was different but not crazy. At the end of the day I was learning slowly but surely that wisdom was not to be despised and welcomed because the truth of the matter is I really do not have to hit every wall. Some I can take the words of others about. Because we all know, fat meat really is greasy.

Scriptural Helps

Job 12:12 NIV Is not wisdom found among the aged? Does not long life bring understanding?

Day 24

Put That in Your Pipe and Smoke It

By now I am sure you can tell that Nanny had a feisty side and she never had a problem with speaking her mind. Never ever, I mean never ever. There were not many times in our relationship that I pushed the envelope with her but that does not mean I didn't at all. I mean after she was a strong willed woman and she was raising a strong willed young woman. At some point those wills were bound to collide, right. Well when they did I knew what was next, Nanny would say her peace and then say, "Now put that in your pipe and smoke it". Here we go again I would think with these colorful cryptic sayings that I would have to go away sit and figure our. Eventually I figured out this meant that she meant what she said but I could do what I wanted to do because I was going to do it anyway. Which for the most part was true, I was a young adult trying to find my own way. When you are young, you think the elders in your life are trying to keep you from something. As you mature you, realize they were but it was only for your good. Sometimes you had to learn to read between the lines and understand they did not want the mistakes of their past to be repeated in your life. SO this was really their way of trying to protect you from you because they did not always do such a good job in their own lives. Selah

Scriptural Helps

Proverbs 16:22 NIV Whoever gives heed to instruction prospers, and blessed is the one that trusts in the Lord

Proverbs 5:1-4 NIV My son, pay attention to my wisdom, listen well to my words of insight, that you may maintain discretion and your lips may preserve knowledge. For the lips of an adulteress drip honey, and her speech is smoother than oil; but in the end she is bitter as gall, sharp as a double-edged sword.

Day 25

God Provides

Growing up there was always a burgundy and white box on the dresser in my grandparent's room that had a numbers on it. I watched my grandfather stand up every Sunday in church and explain that it was "Tithes and Offering" time. The people of God would walk around with those same envelopes and put them in a gold plate. I had loose money for a long time and never inquired about the use of the envelopes. But one day my grandfather was fussing and kept saying, Ella Mae, Ella Mae why aren't my tithes ready"? SO not long after this I ask Nanny what are the envelopes about and she explained about paying God 10% of your earnings. I asked why and she explained because it was in the Bible. She then said to me before meeting my grandfather she really did not subscribe to this tenant before him. Then she began to share how she had seen God provide in ways that she could have never imagined since living by via her husbands obedience to God's covenant. She shared with me just how faithful God has been to them. As I sat and reflected while we were having this conversation, I saw what she was sharing with me. Food was always on the table; utilities were always on, vehicles maintained, family and friends were well and in fact, there was always an overflow for others to receive as well. Now please don't miss understand me and see this as a sun was always shining picture because it rain as well but the good did out weigh the bad because of the faith they held onto that God was a keeper of His word no matter what.

Scriptural Helps

Mark 12:41-44 NIV Jesus sat down opposite the place where the offerings were put and watched the crowd putting their money into the temple treasury. Many rich people threw large amounts. But a poor widow came and put in two very small cooper coins, worth only a few cents. Calling his disciples to him., Jesus said, "Truly I tell you, this poor widow has put more into the treasury than all the others. They all gave out of their wealth, but she, out of her poverty, put in everything- all she had to live on.

Luke 11:42 NIV Woe to you Pharisees, because you give God a tenth of your mint, rue and all other kinds of garden herbs, but you neglect justice and the love of God. You should have practiced the later without leaving the former done.

Day 26

When You Mess Up Go to God and Him Alone

Growing up I attended Catholic School and was a practicing Catholic for a short period. I still attended the Baptist Church that my grandparent's attended when I was with them as well. Jesus and I were rocking it 24-7 those days. I was what they called a "Bible Thumper". Nanny really did not mind me being in a religious setting so much however when she heard about us going to confession and telling the Priest our sins she put her foot down their. Her reply to this was, "When you sin you sin against God alone, so you go to God for yourself not anyone else". Sort of like that old song, "Don't ask my neighbor come to me, never let your friends hang around". King David in the Bible is excellent example of this. Every time he got into a pickle, he went and confessed to God and worked it out between them. No outside interferences, just David and God alone in the tightest places of his life. When I got older and was in my own tight places I always remembered this lesson and went to God and God alone and allowed Him to rework the fabric of my soul.

Scriptural Helps

Psalm 51:4 NIV Against you, you only, have I sinned and done what is evil in your sight; so you are right in your verdict and justified when you judge.

Day 27

Write Your Own Play

After church one day one of the musicians pulled me aside and shared with me that they were writing a play and wanted me to be apart of it. I was so excited to hear this news. I really enjoyed acting. When I got home I was in the kitchen with Nanny and shared what I thought was the most amazing news. Her reply was, "Write your own play". I looked at her like she had two heads when she said that to me. But guess what, "I went to my room, thought about it and began to write my own play. I actually wrote more than one, as well as some poetry pieces. Nanny had a way pushing me to do what I was not sure I could do and do it well. It was like she saw what God gifted me with and knew how to push it out of me when the time was right.

Scriptural Helps

Proverbs 20:5 NIV The purposes of a person's heart are deep waters, but one who has insight draws them out.

Job 42:2 NIV I know that you can do all things; no purpose of yours can be thwarted.

Day 28

I Want You to Be Like Her

January 20, 1993 was the Inauguration of President William Jefferson Clinton. Nanny and I watched the inauguration on television together. This was the first election that I had voted in and was enjoying being apart of the whole process as well as sharing this experience with both my grandparents'. Imagine walking into the polling place and your grandmother announcing, "First time voter, first time voter", I was embarrassed and proud at the same time. So here we sat together watching our new president being sworn in and then not long after and African-American female poet took center stage and began to speak. Her name was Maya Angelou and the poem was entitled, "On the Pulse of Morning". As she stood their tall, erect, proud and so articulate, Nanny turned to me and said, "I want you to be like her". I felt great fear and trepidation take over body when she said that. I was very intimidated by those words. I even thought why would you place such a heavy weight upon me? We never spoke about that again. After Nanny passed I found her Maya Angelou book collection, one in particular, "All God's Children Need Traveling Shoes". I began to read it I began to gain understanding and wisdom. You see the Maya Angelou I saw on January 20, 1993 was not the Maya she had always been. She had traveled life in many shoes, hence had many life experiences that catapulted her to that day. She had been recipient of many wounds that were not her fault, and some self-inflicted. Libraries had become her friend early in life; words close companions although she did not speak much in her younger years. Almost the same as myself, except when I was at school I was very loquacious at least that is what they say. We both had experience sexual assaults in our younger years and later in life. One would say we had a fondness for picking men that were good for right now but not for where we were going. But our art and creative side were always being feed in some aspect of our lives, our passions were very similar if not almost the same. Seeing her as human with a literary superpower leveled the playing field and made me better understand what Nanny was speaking into me in that moment in time. She never said, "I want you to be her", she said, "Be like her"; strong, fearless, woman, African-American, trailblazing, spirited woman who would never give up even when the fight was almost gone out of her. She was s gentle as a summer breeze, as feisty as lioness in the Serengeti, peaceful as a dove and cuddly as a calico kitten.

Scriptural Helps

Psalm 139:14 NIV I praise you because I am fearfully and wonderfully made; your works are wonderful, I know that full well.

Ephesians 2:10 NIV For we are God's handiwork, created in Christ Jesus to do good works, which God prepared in advance fur us to do.

Day 29

That Money Is Burning A Whole In Your Pocket

Riding in the car one day and Nanny begins to share with me about an annuity that she had some information about and was suggesting that I invest in at that time. I was all of about 21/22 and she was having a conversation with me about being 59 ½ and penalties and all. At that age 59 ½ is 100 years away and I am not giving any one that much of my money that I just started making in the first place. Didn't she know I needed fly clothes, a car and a house? Retirement we can think about later. Nanny said I was spending money like it was going to burn a hole in my pocket that I needed to start thinking about later now. I did not start investing then but slowly but surely her words began to sink in and I made small changes over time. I became a mother and 59 ½ and my legacy became more important. I started making investments and planning for my future. She planted a very important seed in my life at young age that I was at first resistant to but eventually fell in line with. Money is a tool, not a God and we need to have a healthier perspective on how we view it and use it. We should do that wisely.

Scriptural Helps

Proverbs 21:20 NIV The wise store up choice food and olive oil, but fools gulp theirs down

Proverbs 13:11 NIV Dishonest money dwindles away, but whoever gathers money little by little makes it grow

Day 30

Without God I Am Nothing

In the kitchen is where I would hear these words ringing out, as Nanny would sing them. It was her anthem for her life. In good times and in the not so good times she still stood strong with this declaration. If you would you could say it was her legacy that she left to me and all those around her. God was her everything and I came to know Him in that way for myself. You see Nanny gave me many gifts but the gift of her faith in God was the greatest that she could ever give and she knew that. It would be what would get me through my darkest days and loneliest nights. It would be what I needed survive her being diagnosed with cancer, watching and her suffer and then God call her home to be with Him. It is what gave me the strength and courage to parent an amazing daughter all the way up until today. It is that faith that I passed down to my daughter as well. As far as I am concerned, it is our legacy and one that I am the most proud of.

Scriptural Helps

2 Timothy 1:5-6 NIV I am reminded of your sincere faith, which first lived in your grandmother Lois and in your mother Eunice and, I am persuaded, now lives in you also. For this reason I remind you to fan into flame the gift of God, which is in you through the laying on of my hands.

Ramona M. Gaines is the founder and CEO of Styllwaters' Café Inc. and Styllwaters' Ministries a non-profit-organization that provides a venue for Christian artist to perform and network. The Styllwaters' Story, Ramona's first book is the inspirational story of life, and passion that lead her to establish the Styllwaters' Café.

A seasoned entrepreneur, Gaines operates Parent Kids Network, which specializes in restoring and transforming the lives of parents and children by instilling family values and offering structural guidance that not only builds strong families but strong communities.

As the visionary of Movement is Medicine, Gaines not only seeks to inspire others but create a movement through a compilation of stories about how a commitment to move daily can become the medicine to overcome spiritual, physical and emotional challenges. The powerful series includes Movement Is Medicine: Volume I, Women Determined to Rise: Volume II, Men Determined to Break Free: Volume III, and The Seasons of Love: Volume IV, parallels Chicken Soup for the Soul as it takes readers on a journey of spiritual, physical and emotional transformation. Gaines' who is a storyteller by nature has recently launched a line of children's book series called, "Nanny and Me". It is a collection of stories of her summers and other special holiday's that she spent with her Nanny and the traditions of faith, family and her love of creating great food.

A native of Philadelphia, Pennsylvania, Gaines attended Millersville University where she studied Radio and Television Broadcasting. Gaines also attended Manna Bible School and she is certified Trauma Specialist at The Institute of Family Professionals at Lakeside Education Network.

Author Ramona M. Gaines can be reached at visionaryrmg@gmail.com

www.visionaryramonamgaines.com

Made in the USA
Las Vegas, NV
18 December 2024

14739743R00098